GETTING TO GRIPS WITH GRAMMAR

Punctuation

Commas, Full Stops, and Question Marks

Anita Ganeri

www.raintreepublishers.co.uk
Visit our website to find out
more information about
Raintree books.

To order:
☎ Phone 0845 6044371
🖨 Fax +44 (0) 1865 312263
✉ Email myorders@raintreepublishers.co.uk

Customers from outside the UK please telephone +44 1865 312262

Raintree is an imprint of Capstone Global Library Limited,
a company incorporated in England and Wales having its
registered office at 7 Pilgrim Street, London, EC4V 6LB
– Registered company number: 6695582

Edited by Daniel Nunn, Rebecca Rissman, and Sian Smith
Designed by Joanna Hinton-Malivoire
Picture research by Tracy Cummins
Original illustrations © Capstone Global Library
Illustrated by Joanna Hinton-Malivoire
Production by Eirian Griffiths
Originated by Capstone Global Library Ltd
Printed in China

ISBN 978 1 406 23241 7 (hardback)
15 14 13 12 11
10 9 8 7 6 5 4 3 2 1

ISBN 978 1 406 23248 6 (paperback)
16 15 14 13 12
10 9 8 7 6 5 4 3 2 1

British Library Cataloguing in Publication Data
Ganeri, Anita, 1961-
Punctuation: commas, full stops, and question marks.
(Getting to grips with grammar)
421.1-dc22
A full catalogue record for this book is available from the
British Library.

Acknowledgements
We would like to thank the following for permission to reproduce
photographs and artworks: istockphoto pp.13 (© Derek Latta),
19 (© Murat Taşcı), 23 (© Anna Jurkovska); Shutterstock pp.5
(© gosphotodesign), 6 (© Elliot Westacott), 7 (© Harald Lueder),
10 (© HitToon.Com), 11 (© Odin M. Eidskrem), 12 (© Stayer), 14
(© Juriah Mosin), 15 (© onime), 16 (© Ivan Kruk), 17 (© Tiago
Jorge da Silva Estima), 18 (© Zurijeta), 20 (© Cherry-Merry),
22 (© ericlefrancais), 24 (© Mark Stout Photography), 25 (©
gosphotodesign), 26 (© Lorelyn Medina), 27 (© Podfoto), 29 (©
charles taylor).

Every effort has been made to contact copyright holders
of material reproduced in this book. Any omissions will
be rectified in subsequent printings if notice is given to the
publisher.

Contents

Some words are shown in bold, **like this**.
You can find them in the glossary on page 31.

What is grammar?

Grammar is a set of rules that helps you to write and speak a language. Grammar is important because it helps people to understand each other.

lunch. Yesterday, had for pasta I

Without grammar, this **sentence** doesn't make sense.

This book is about **punctuation**. Punctuation is a set of marks and signs that you use in writing. They help readers to understand the meaning of the words.

Yesterday, I had pasta for lunch.

Grammar turns the jumbled-up words into a sentence.

What is punctuation?

Punctuation is used to break up words and **sentences**. It makes writing clearer and easier to understand.

> **I took my dog for a walk.**

. is a **full stop**. It marks the end of the sentence.

In speech, people can change the way their words sound to show what they mean. In writing, punctuation helps to do this job.

Punctuation marks

The marks and signs used in **punctuation** are called punctuation marks. Each mark does a different job.

These are the main punctuation marks.

. **full stop**

? **question mark**

! **exclamation mark**

, **comma**

" " **speech marks**

' **apostrophe**

Thousands of years ago, people did not leave gaps between words. Later, they started leaving spaces and using punctuation marks.

ifyoudontleavespaceswriting lookssilly

Without punctuation, writing is hard to understand.

Spot the punctuation marks

Look at the two **sentences** below. Can you spot all the **punctuation** marks?

The witch had a cat, a bat, and a broomstick.

Which is the way to the station?

In the first sentence, there are **commas** and a **full stop**. In the second sentence, there is a **question mark**.

Can you tell the difference between these two sentences?

We ate chocolate, cake, and ice cream.

We ate chocolate cake and ice cream.

Remember, punctuation marks make the meaning clearer. But you can also change the meaning by putting punctuation marks in different places.

Capital letters

Capital letters are **upper-case letters**. These are letters, such as A, B, C, D, E, and so on. You always put a capital letter at the beginning of a **sentence**.

This sentence begins with a capital 'T'.

This tiger has a long tail.

The names of people and places are **proper nouns**. They also begin with capital letters. You also use a capital 'I' when you talk about yourself.

> **My friend Lizzy likes dancing.**
>
> **My friends and I went shopping.**

'Lizzy' is a person's name, so it begins with a capital letter. You always use a capital 'I' to talk about yourself.

Full stops

You use a **full stop** at the end of a **sentence**. It shows that the sentence has finished.

I went swimming with my sister.

This sentence ends with a full stop.

I watched a programme on the TV. It was very funny.

The full stops show you when to pause.

Read the two sentences above. You take a short break when you see a full stop.

Question marks

Sometimes, you use a **question mark** at the end of a **sentence**. It shows that the sentence is asking a question.

Have you seen my gloves?

This sentence ends with a question mark.

Look at the two sentences below. Which of them needs a question mark at the end?

Where is the zoo

I like the lions best

The first sentence asks a question, so it needs a question mark.

Exclamation marks

Sometimes, you use an **exclamation mark** at the end of a **sentence**. It shows when you feel strongly about something or when you are surprised.

My birthday party was brilliant!

This sentence ends with an exclamation mark.

Look at the two sentences below. Which of them needs an exclamation mark at the end?

She felt tired and went to sleep

I couldn't believe it

The second sentence shows strong feeling, so it needs an exclamation mark.

Commas

A **comma** is a **punctuation** mark that you can use in different ways. You can use commas to break up the words in a list.

I go to gym on Monday, Tuesday, and Friday.

Commas are used to break up 'Monday', 'Tuesday', and 'Friday'.

My best friends are Elsa, Karim, and Lucas.

My best friends are Elsa, Karim and Lucas.

You don't need a comma before 'and Lucas' but you can use one if you like.

You don't need to use a comma before the word 'and' when it is used in a list, but some people do. Look at the **sentences** above.

More commas

You can also use **commas** to break up long **sentences**. You take a little pause when you see the comma. This makes long sentences easier to read.

The comma breaks up the long sentence.

I wanted to buy a new pair of shoes, but I didn't have enough money.

Commas can be used to separate out information in a long sentence, too.

The boy, who was wearing a red T-shirt, ran down the path.

The commas around 'who was wearing a red T-shirt' make the sentence easier to read.

Speech marks

Speech marks are used to show the words that someone has spoken. They are also called **inverted commas**.

"Lunch is ready!" said Mum.

You use speech marks to show what someone has said.

Sam said, "I'm not hungry."

Can you see the pair of speech marks in this **sentence**?

You always use speech marks in pairs.
One set is put before the spoken words.
One set is put after the spoken words.

Apostrophes

An **apostrophe** looks like a flying **comma**. You can use apostrophes to show that you have left out some of the letters in a word.

It's time we went to bed.

In this sentence, 'it is' is written as 'it's'.

You use apostrophes to join words together. This makes your writing sound more like talking. It also sounds friendlier.

'Could' and 'not' join together to make 'couldn't'.

I couldn't find my school bag.

More apostrophes

You can also use **apostrophes** to show that someone owns something. If there is only one owner, the apostrophe goes at the end of the word. Then you add 's'. If there are lots of owners, you put the apostrophe after the 's'.

This means that the cat belongs to the girl.

This is the girl's cat.

These are the boys' coats.

This means that the coats belong to the boys.

These are the children's toys.

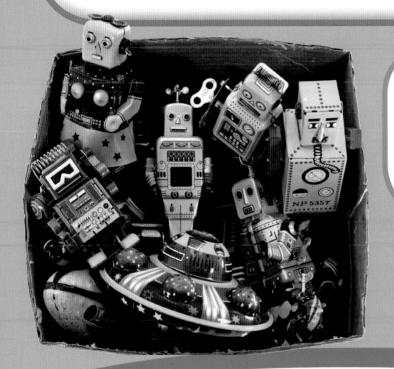

This means that the toys belong to the children.

If there are lots of owners but the word does not end in an 's' already, you put the apostrophe at the end of the word. Then you add 's'.

Add the punctuation

Which **punctuation** marks and **capital letters** need to be added below?

i found some buried treasure

how many people are called emma

im afraid of the dark but im fine if i have a torch

remember to brush your teeth said dad

Answers:
I found some buried treasure!
How many people are called Emma?
I'm afraid of the dark, but if I have a torch.
"Remember to brush your teeth!" said Dad.

Glossary

apostrophe mark that shows where letters have been left out of a word or that someone owns something

capital letter upper-case letter, such as A, B, C, D, E

comma mark that breaks up the words in a sentence

exclamation mark mark at the end of a sentence to show a strong feeling

full stop mark that shows the end of a sentence

grammar a set of rules that helps you speak or write clearly

inverted commas marks that show the words someone has spoken. They are also called speech marks.

proper noun the name of a person, place, or thing

punctuation marks and signs you use in writing to make the meaning clear

question mark mark at the end of a sentence to show a question

sentence group of words that makes sense on its own

speech marks marks that show the words someone has spoken. They are also called inverted commas.

upper-case letter capital letter, such as A, B, C, D, E

Find out more

Books

Go Further with Grammar, Ruth Thomson (Belitha Press, 2004)
Grammar Ray series, Andrew Carter (Evans Brothers, 2009)
Punctuation: The Write Stuff!, Mary Budzik (Kingfisher, 2010)
The Perfect (Pop-Up) Punctuation Book, Kate Petty (Bodley Head, 2006)

Websites

www.bbc.co.uk/schools/ks2bitesize/english/spelling_grammar/
Find out more about punctuation and test your skills by playing a game.

www.bbc.co.uk/schools/ks1bitesize/literacy/punctuation/index.shtml
Help two characters talk to aliens by correcting the aliens' punctuation and capital letters.

Index